Featherstone

Series editor ALISTAIR BRYCE-CLEGG

50 fantastic ideas for small world provocations

JUDIT HORVATH

Featherstone
An imprint of Bloomsbury Publishing Plc

50 Bedford Square
London
WC1B 3DP
UK

1385 Broadway
New York
NY 10018
USA

www.bloomsbury.com

First published 2017

British Library Cataloguing-in-Publication Data
A catalogue record for this book is available from the British Library.

ISBN:
PB 978-1-4729-3836-7
ePDF 978-1-4729-3837-4

Library of Congress Cataloging-in-Publication Data
A catalogue record for this book is available from the Library of Congress.

10 9 8 7 6 5 4 3 2 1

Printed and bound in India by Replika Press Pvt Ltd.

Contents

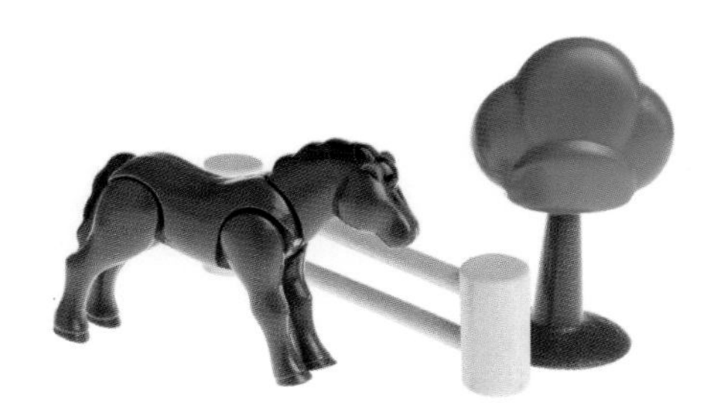

Introduction

The aims of the book

Small world play provides the opportunity to create a real life or imaginative scene for children to engage with using miniatures and representatives of real objects, animals and people. Small world provocations are usually set up for a certain theme that is relevant and meaningful to the children at the time. They often include a sensory element (water, sand, dry pasta, grains, leaves, pebbles etc) which provides additional layers to the play and learning. Apart from being fun for the children, small world play also offers a wealth of development opportunities for:

- language development, literacy – children begin to play with their voices to personalise characters and they will actively, see, prepare and use labels, texts and letters, and draw on their story-telling skills
- problem solving and basic maths – setting up scenes together, working through issues between characters, planning and counting elements and working out problems within the scene itself will help children to reason, negotiate, express and listen
- developing individual and social play skills – small worlds with their open sequence of play provide opportunities for children of different ages and stages to play according to their individual needs
- emotional development – trying and testing feelings and reactions to real life events
- understanding the world around them – by replaying and retelling stories from real life children's knowledge and understanding will deepen, providing them with a better ability to express pieces of information learnt through play.

The main aim of this book is to provide ideas on how to set up small world provocations for children to act out thoughts, feelings and events, and re-enact stories they know of, as a safe framework to test and process their own individual inner world.

The structure of the book

The structure of this book is based on ideas for different small world provocations set up in various settings that would fit different types and levels of the curriculum, providing a colourful selection to suit different ages, stages and interests.

The activities are divided into five groups, based on the type of resource that contains the small world.

- Sand play: The first section describes activities that are sand based and can be set up in various sand trays. Sand lends itself to small worlds as a versatile base, acting as earth, desert, the moon surface and so on.
- Shallow trays: The second section lists ten activities that can be created in shallow trays, so the children have easy access to changing and personalising the small world, reflecting their ideas.
- Water world: The third section contains water based small worlds. With its instant sensory appeal these small worlds have the potential to engage the youngest children.
- Cereal box play: The fourth group of activities are organised around an easily sourced prop, cereal boxes. These often involve the children in drawing and planning.
- Free form play: The last ten small worlds are free form setups, with no particular borders, so can easily be played as simple tabletop activities.

Within the five groups, each activity description contains the list of resources required, titled 'What you need'. The activities are clearly explained step-by-step, with easy-to-follow instructions under the section 'What to do', including suggested extensions and variations for ensuring flexible provision to fit for different settings, children and individual needs. The section titled 'What's in it for the children?' describes the educational aims and learning opportunities of the activity. Additional ideas for similar activities are provided for occasions when there is an instant need to take the learning further or to change the direction of the activity to maintain the children's interest. The activity descriptions also highlight some observation questions that offer brief suggestions on how to follow the children's learning effectively, and to enrich their learning in the future.

For some activities adults will need to carry out certain tasks adhering to the Health & Safety procedures in place within their childcare setting.

Why are children drawn to small world play?

Small world play, regardless of the details of the setup, is an engaging, free and exciting form of role play that can be easily manipulated and is very inclusive for young children. Within these scenarios children can relive experiences that might appear scary, difficult or questionable, and process them at their own level, whatever life is bringing their way. They also enjoy the freedom of creating miniature worlds, where they can appear to be the controlling 'big' people. Being in charge brings its own questions, challenges, joys and rewards, which is excellent practice for social behaviour. Children's imaginations are their greatest strength, the driving force behind all their play processes and the motivation for all kinds of learning. Small worlds are the perfect place to explore the answer to the usual questions: 'What if...?', 'Why...?' and so on.

Providing successful small world play

Children from a very early age can engage in (simple) small world play and start telling their own stories through their play. Symbolic play starts to emerge by using an object as something else, and parallel to that, language starts to develop. Successful small world play can move children along greatly in their learning.

- Decide on the theme: chose a subject based on what the child has experienced or has an interest in.
- Collect the materials in advance: be inspired by various places, including the toy box, the kitchen, the garden or anywhere else within reach. Include the children in setting up the scene, as this is part of the fun. Children love to be involved and hunt for items they might want to use, especially when popular themes are chosen.
- Try to add at least one sensory element to the play (like sand, water, play dough, clay, grass, straw, uncooked rice, rocks, even a piece of wood…) as children primarily learn through their senses.
- Choose the containing resource carefully, so it is not limiting but instead elevates the play. Sometimes children also need their small world to be limitless.
- Set the provocation keeping the users in mind. The younger the children are, the simpler the small world should be, whereas you can set up quite elaborate scenes for older children.
- Play along and cater for everyone, remember that all children are different. Some children need a little help getting started; others can play independently.

The pond

Sand tray

What you need:

- Sand tray/container
- A bowl of water
- Soil and sand
- Pebbles, shells
- Moss, leaves, sticks
- Fish/water world toys

What to do:

1. Discuss the scene that will be set.
2. Ask the children to make a layout plan for the small world, eg. by drawing sketches.
3. Place the sand tray/container safely on a stand, table or on the ground.
4. Place a bowl in the middle of the tray and fill it with water to create the pond.
5. Work alongside the children as they play and encourage them to act out stories and use a wide vocabulary to explore the characteristics of their play figures.
6. Encourage the children to think imaginatively and to find items to represent characters and other objects, for example, a twig from the outdoor area to use as driftwood.

What's in it for the children?

Children will be able to build play environments, tell stories involving key characters and sequencing events, work alone or co-operatively, discuss their ideas and negotiate roles with others, use language to link ideas and recreate experiences, explore concepts of space and size, make maps and plans, become deeply involved in play, and develop ideas and understanding over a period of time.

Taking it forward

- Act out pond related stories such as *The Pig in the Pond* by Martin Waddell or *The Pirates of the Pond* by Francis Keene.
- Create a thematic scene based on a well-known rhyme such as 'Five Little Speckled Frogs'.

Observation questions

- Can the children work as part of a group?
- Do the children show an understanding of basic concepts?

The forest

Sand tray

What you need:

- Sand tray/container
- Soil and sand
- Moss, leaves, sticks, bark pieces
- Brown playdough or clay
- Fern leaves and other dry plants
- Pine cones
- Plastic forest animals
- Real grass
- Logs

What to do:

1. Discuss the scene that will be set and ask the children to contribute their ideas.
2. Place the sand tray/container safely on a table or on the ground.
3. Create the ground features using your fingers to partition up the different parts of the forest.
4. Create a canopy, an understorey and a forest floor layer, by placing different sized logs standing up to achieve a 3D effect. Scatter around fresh and dry plants for the forest floor.
5. Add small details such as moss leaves, bark and toy animals.
6. Work alongside the children as they play and encourage them to act out stories and/or situations. Encourage the children to think imaginatively when representing the roles and characters in their own story with the objects found in the small world.

What's in it for the children?

Children will be able to creatively process events, and by providing experiences for many of their senses (vision, touch, smell) the learning will be deeper and more meaningful.

Taking it forward

- Create different types of forest small worlds, such as a European forest, rain forest, winter forest etc.

Observation questions

- Can the children tell or retell a story?
- Do the children show an understanding of representation?

Beach patrol

Sand tray

What you need:

- Sand tray/container
- Sand
- Blue card
- Paper in different colours
- Glue or tape
- Juice boxes and straws
- Scissors
- Shells, pebbles
- Play figures and sealife animals

What to do:

1. Discuss the children's past experiences of beaches. For younger children include photos to remind them.
2. Place the sand tray/container safely on a table or on the ground.
3. Push the sand towards one side, and cover the other side with blue card or with blue paper coloured by the children.
4. Cut out beach items such as a towel or a bucket and spade and lay them on the sandy side.
5. Create simple boats: place an empty juice box on its side horizontally and push the straw through gently (so it doesn't go all the way through to the other side). Cut triangles out of paper for the sail, and secure them to your straw mast. Sit plastic figures on the top. Put these on the blue 'water' side of the scene.
6. Add fine detail with shells, pebbles, extra figures and sealife.
7. Work alongside the children as they play and encourage them to act out different stories and scenarios.

What's in it for the children?

Children can explore how humans encounter wildlife in certain places and why it's important to respect natural places.

Taking it forward

- Add 'litter' such as paper pieces, plastic cup pieces etc. and organise a 'beach clean' movement.
- Create a wildlife observation station and add natural elements to the small world scene such as dry seaweed, beach sand, feathers etc.

Observation questions

- Do the children show an interest in imaginative play?
- Does the small world play influence the children's usual attitudes?

Dakar rally

Sand tray

What you need:

- Sand tray/container
- Sand
- Pieces of rocks and small pebbles
- Toy rally cars, mini trucks
- Small pieces of green tissue paper (optional)

What's in it for the children?

Children can learn about various aspects of the wider world, for example competitive sports and the joys and dangers of different activities.

Taking it forward

- Give children the map of the real Dakar rally, provide pictures of the competition and ask them to recreate real scenes.
- Create scenes with different weather conditions.

Observation questions

- Do the children use their imaginations to engage with unknown, unusual scenes?
- Do they notice new things, do they note new information?

What to do:

1. Discuss the scene that will be set. Explain to children what rally sport means, and if possible play a video (YouTube) about the Dakar rally.
2. Place the sand tray/container safely on a table or on the ground.
3. Scatter sand around in the bottom of the tray, then create the ground features: make a road by using fingers to partition the sand, add rocks and tissue paper as the landscape and plants.
4. Place the cars within the scene.
5. Work alongside the children as they play and encourage them to act out the stories, remembering what they saw on the video.
6. Encourage children to think imaginatively and fully explore the space.

Desert island

Sand tray

What you need:

- Sand tray/container
- Sand
- Corn grit
- Pebbles
- Sticks
- Green wool
- Desert figures

What to do:

1. Discuss the story and the scene that will be set and show the children pictures of a desert. Talk about the special features of the setting and how dry and hot it would be.
2. Place the sand tray/container safely on a table or on the ground.
3. Scatter sand in the bottom of the tray, then cover the majority with corn grit.
4. Create the landscape features.
5. Add play characters and work alongside the children as they play to encourage them.

What's in it for the children?

Small world play offers the children access to both independent and social play skills. This is an important time to gather thoughts and test ideas, with or without input from others. The play skills are vital in gaining self-confidence and self-awareness.

Taking it forward

- Create a realistic desert experience by carefully blowing across the top of the small world with a hairdryer to create a sand storm.
- Encourage children to discuss the characteristics of human life in the desert, use books to aid the discussion.

Observation questions

- Can the children express their ideas?
- Do the children play independently?

The land before time

Sand tray

What you need:

- Sand tray/container
- Soil
- Sand, pebbles
- Moss, leaves, sticks
- Green wool (optional)
- Dry twigs, tree bark
- Dinosaur toys

What to do:

1. Discuss the story and the scene that will be set and ask the children to create a plan or draw sketches.
2. Place the sand tray/container safely on a table or on the ground.
3. Scatter sand and soil in the bottom of the tray, then add the ground features: twigs, bark etc. For a forest effect add bunches of green wool.
4. Add the plastic dinosaurs or make paper dinosaurs, drawn by the children.
5. Work alongside the children as they play and encourage them to act out stories.
6. Encourage children to think imaginatively and to find items to represent characters and other objects, for example, a twig from the outdoor area to use as a tree.

What's in it for the children?

Children are imagining, and while doing so they talk out loud and use their vocabulary in a variety of contexts. Whilst playing, imagination stretches the limits of their knowledge, whether the play is independent or as part of a group.

Taking it forward

- Act out popular dinosaur stories such as *How Do Dinosaurs Say Good Night?* by Jane Yolen, *Saturday Night at the Dinosaur Stomp* by Carol Diggory Shields and so on.

Observation questions

- Do the children have some understanding of time and history?
- Do the children actively engage?

Space and moon

Sand tray

What you need:

- Sand tray/container
- Sand
- Aluminium foil
- Cardboard tube
- Coloured card
- Glue
- Pebbles, small rocks
- Play people figures

What's in it for the children?

In small world play children need to demonstrate adaptation and negotiation skills. Children's problem-solving skills will develop as they engage in scenarios which will often change as they play.

Taking it forward

- Add extra features such as battery operated tealights, or cover the whole tray and play in the dark.
- Create a set of small world planets to play with.

Observation questions

- Can the children adapt to new situations?
- Do the children express their emotions through their play?

What to do:

1. Discuss the scene that will be set and look at images together.
2. Ask the children to make a layout plan for the small world, eg. by making a sketch.
3. Make the spaceship by wrapping the cardboard tube in aluminium foil, then gluing strips of card onto the bottom for the legs.
4. Make the astronauts by wrapping plastic figures in aluminium foil.
5. Place the sand tray/container safely on a stand, table or on the ground.
6. Create the base by placing pebbles, small rocks and pieces of aluminium foil on the ground.
7. Add the figures and the spaceship.
8. Work alongside the children as they play and encourage them to act out stories.

Autumn senses

Sand tray

What you need:

- **Sand tray/container**
- **Soil and sand**
- **Dry and fresh nuts, seeds and plant parts**
- **Dry leaves**
- **A mushroom** (optional)
- **Paper and colouring pencils**

What to do:

1. Discuss the scene that will be set and talk about the features of autumn.
2. Ask the children to make a layout plan for the small world, for example draw sketches using autumnal colours.
3. Children can colour paper in yellow, red, brown and orange to create a ground cover for the scene.
4. Place the sand tray/container safely on a stand, table or on the ground.
5. Scatter the various plant pieces around the sand tray and encourage children to touch, listen to and smell all the items. Remind them not to taste any!
6. Work alongside the children as they play and encourage them to act out their stories.

What's in it for the children?

Children will be able to explore the world through their senses and gain information about their environment through touch, hearing, smell and vision. The variety of experiences will enrich their ability to describe their feelings and attitudes towards their immediate and wider environment.

Taking it forward

- Create a small world provocation for each of the seasons in turn, gathering suitable natural objects.
- Play a guessing game by blind folding a child, then making noises with the objects (such as shaking some nuts in the palm, rubbing a dry leaf etc.) and encouraging children to guess what made the noise.

Observation questions

- Do the children use a variety of senses to explore their environment?
- Can the children describe their experiences?

Vegetable garden

Sand tray

What you need:

- Sand tray/container
- Soil and sand
- Pebbles, shells
- Moss, leaves, sticks
- Real vegetables
- Toy figures

What to do:

1. Discuss the scene that will be set.
2. Ask the children to share their experiences about fresh vegetables (such as what do they smell like, why they are good for us to eat etc.).
3. Place the sand tray/container safely on a stand, table or on the ground.
4. Cover the sand with clean earth.
5. Create sections of the garden and its different types of produce, such as cucumbers, tomatoes, herbs etc., then place the toy 'gardener' within the garden.
6. Work alongside the children as they play and encourage them to explore the vegetables and build play situations with their newly gained experiences.

What's in it for the children?

The goal of this activity is for children to act out ideas from real life and re-enact stories they know in play situations.

Taking it forward

- Create a play herb garden with real herbs.
- Create a thematic, foreign gardens with vegetables from different cultures such as Spanish, African, Caribbean etc.

Observation questions

- Can the children retell their previous story experiences through the small world play scene?
- Do the children show interest in the cultural aspects?

House on the rocks

Sand tray

What you need:

- Sand tray/container
- Sand
- Pebbles and small rocks
- Building blocks
- Play people figures

What to do:

1. Discuss the scene that will be set. Tell the traditional story of the wise and foolish man who built his house on the sand and the rocks, and then talk about opposites.
2. Place the sand tray/container safely on a stand, table or on the ground.
3. Place sand on one side and pieces of rocks on the other.
4. Build a house out of small building blocks and place them on the side with the rocks.
5. Place a handful of blocks scattered around on the sandy side.
6. Work alongside the children as they play and encourage them to act out the story.
7. Add play people and carry out imaginary conversations to discuss the events (why did the house go 'splat', what could be done to avoid it etc.).

What's in it for the children?

Children will be able to understand opposites. Older children will learn about how decisions and choices can affect the circumstances of our lives.

Taking it forward

- Organise other small worlds with opposites such as a town with small and tall buildings.
- Ask all of the children individually to set the scene based on their favourite nursery rhyme.

Observation questions

- Can the children understand basic concepts through the small world?
- Do the children follow storylines?

The farm

Shallow trays

What you need:

- Shallow tray
- Soil
- Hay
- Wood chippings
- Green wool
- Seeds
- Sticks
- Play people and farm animal figures
- Toy farm accessories such as tractors (optional)

What to do:

1. Discuss the scene that will be set, ideally following a farm visit or after reading farm-themed books with the children.
2. Divide the children into small groups.
3. Place a shallow tray safely on a stand, table or on the ground for each group.
4. Encourage the children to create partitions with sticks then fill each section with a different type of bedding for a variety of animals, such as soil for the pig sty, hay for the horse stable, seeds for the chicken coop etc.
5. Add the animals and people.
6. Work alongside the children as they play and encourage them to act out farm-related nursery rhymes.

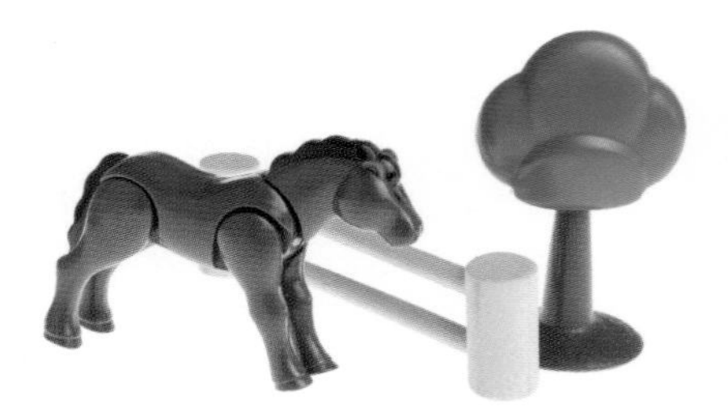

What's in it for the children?

Children will be able to act out familiar and popular nursery rhymes. Retelling stories and recollecting past experiences will help their language development and in turn strengthen their social abilities and confidence.

Taking it forward

- Make a sensory farm by adding blue food colouring to water to make a tinted pond, brown vanilla scented playdough as mud and real grass.

Observation questions

- Can the children reorganise the scene using their own initiative?
- Do the children share the toys?

Evolution

Shallow trays

What you need:

- **Shallow tray**
- **Soil**
- **Stones**
- **White pebbles** (as dinosaur eggs)
- **Black or grey felt tip pen**
- **Different types of mini dinosaurs**
- **Animal figures such as a bird, a mammal, a fish etc.**
- **Magnifiers**

What to do:

1. Explain the concept of evolution, and then discuss the scene that will be set.
2. Make crack-like lines on the white pebbles with a felt tip pen to represent eggs.
3. Place a shallow tray safely on a stand, table or on the ground.
4. Scatter a mixture of soil and stones on the bottom and organise a selection of the homemade eggs around the tray.
5. Place the mini dinosaurs in the tray, and a representative animal from each class of vertebrates (birds, mammals, fish, reptiles, amphibians) outside the tray.
6. Work alongside the children as they play and encourage them to observe the characteristics of the animals outside the tray and guess which dinosaur they have evolved from.

What's in it for the children?

Children are perfect amateur scientists as the questions 'What is that?' and 'Where did that come from?' come as part of their natural curiosity.

During the evolution small world play you may have conversation with children such as 'What's that?', 'It's a bird.' 'Where did it come from?', 'From a dinosaur that was well-adapted to changing conditions millions of years ago.' Providing thought-provoking answers such as this will encourage the children to explore further.

Taking it forward

- Set scenes according to a variety of historical periods such as the ice age, seed-producing gymnosperm where forests dominate the land, the mammoths of the Cenozoic era etc.

Observation questions

- Do the children have an understanding of the concept of time?
- Do the children notice small details?

Arctic world

Shallow trays

What you need:

- Shallow tray
- Aluminium foil
- Rice and/or flour
- Tissue paper, white feathers, polystyrene pieces, egg cartoon
- Small soft or plastic arctic animals

What's in it for the children?

Children's creativity will develop through their efforts to create stories using toys and other items to represent new things. Their physical abilities and their fine motor skills will become stronger through arranging and ordering small objects. Their knowledge and understanding will widen when exploring different worlds, names and types of animals, animal behaviours, food and habitats.

Taking it forward

- Add shaving foam, fresh white rose petals, white playdough, marshmallows and pieces of white soap for a sensory arctic scene.
- Add some ice cubes for exploration.

Observation questions

- Can the children control the small world figures to express their thoughts?
- Do the children engage with the small world?

What to do:

1. Discuss the scene that will be set and talk about the features of a cold and icy place.
2. Place the shallow tray safely on a stand, a table or the ground.
3. Cover the bottom of the tray with aluminium foil.
4. Scatter rice and flour on it to represent snow.
5. Use a selection of white items to create the arctic landscape.
6. Encourage the children to create different scenes with the animals.
7. Work alongside the children as they play and encourage them to act out stories.

Alien landing

Shallow trays

What you need:

- Shallow tray
- Paper and pencil
- Flour
- Baby oil
- Glitter
- Plastic or paper plates
- Aluminium foil
- Play people figures
- Doll house furniture

Taking it forward

- Video the alien landing.

Observation questions

- Can the children express their ideas and views?
- Do the children accept, tolerate and support the ideas of their peers?

What to do:

1. Discuss the scene that will be set: imagine what would happen if aliens took over the world…
2. Create the moon dust by mixing three parts flour with one part baby oil and glitter.
3. Draw and cut out aliens.
4. Make the alien ship by covering a paper plate with aluminium foil.
5. Place a shallow tray safely on a stand, table or on the ground.
6. Create a home scene with doll's house furniture and scatter moon dust over it.
7. Encourage the children to organise the scene and land their aliens.
8. Record the children's stories and photograph their scenes to create a personalised book.

What's in it for the children?

The activity will nurture children's creativity, imagination and language. It will invite and encourage children to express and negotiate their ideas and to act as part of a group.

Incy Wincy Spider

Shallow trays

What you need:

- Shallow tray
- Duct tape or coloured tape
- Silver glitter
- Guttering pipes (or other plastic tubing)
- Cardboard tubes
- Felt tip pens
- Wire
- Spray bottle (optional)
- *Incy Wincy Spider* nursery rhyme book

What to do:

1. Sing and read the 'Incy Wincy Spider' story together and then discuss the scene that will be set.
2. Make spiders: cut the cardboard tube into three rings to make three spider bodies. Next, ask the children to draw on the spiders' eyes and colour in the rest of the tube however they like. Then, chop the wire into twenty four roughly even pieces, and pierce four pieces through each side of each spider's body. Bend the wire inside tube so it is flat against the lining, then secure the ends with sticky tape. You now have three bendy-legged spiders!
3. Place a shallow tray safely on a stand, table or on the ground.
4. Create a spider web design on the top of the tray, securing the tape on the rim of the tray.
5. Scatter glitter across the web to represent water drops.
6. Stand the pieces of guttering within the spider web, to represent Incy Wincy's water spout.
7. Encourage the children to act out the story and change parts of it for fun.
8. Add rain by spraying water on the spiders.

Health & Safety

Ensure the children are always supervised while handling the wire and check for sharp edges.

What's in it for the children?

Children will be able to act out familiar and popular nursery rhymes. Retelling stories, recollecting past experiences will help their language development and in turn strengthen their social abilities and confidence.

Taking it forward

- Make a scene for other versions of 'Incy Wincy Spider' such as:

Incy Wincy Spider climbed up the trees.
Down came the snow and made poor Incy freeze.
Out came the sunshine, and melted all the snow
So Incy Wincy Spider had another go.

(use tree bark for the scene instead of guttering and flour for snow)

Incy Wincy Spider climbed up the stair.
Whoosh went the wind and blew him in the air.
Out came the sunshine, no longer did it blow
So Incy Wincy Spider had another go.

(use small building blocks for stairs instead of guttering, create wind with a fan)

Observation questions

- Can the children accept changes when facing versions of a familiar text?
- Do the children share the toys?

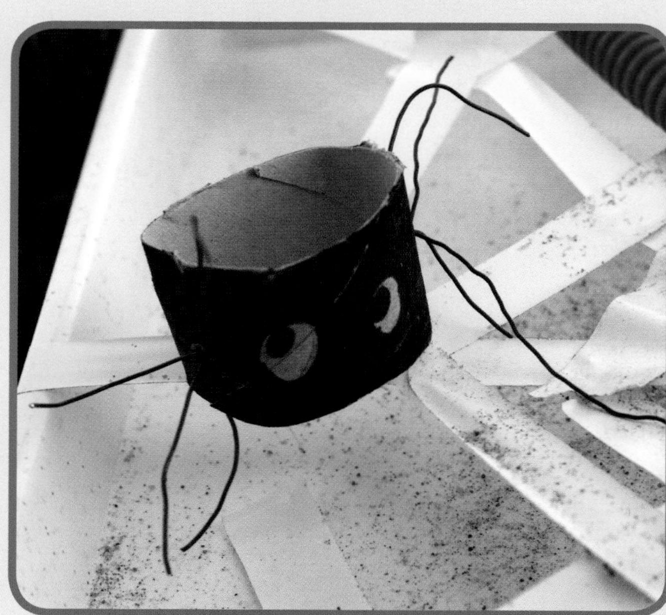

Animal painting

Shallow trays

What you need:

- Shallow tray
- White paper
- Sticky tack
- Selection of small plastic animals
- Paint in trays

What to do:

1. Cover the bottom of a shallow tray with white paper, secure it with sticky tack so it is easy to replace.
2. Place the tray safely on a stand, table or on the ground.
3. Place small trays of paint next to the children.
4. Provide a variety of animals.
5. Work alongside the children as they play and encourage them to create unique patterns dipping the animals into the paint and making footprints of their animals on the base paper.

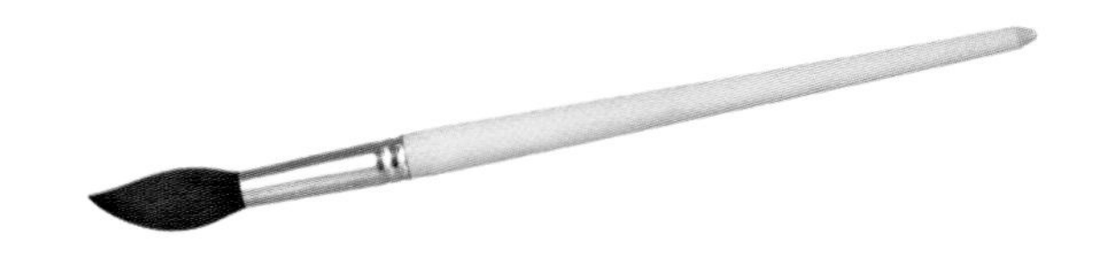

What's in it for the children?

Children will be able to explore and create patterns and shapes.

Taking it forward

- Provide cut vegetables for vegetable printing.
- Select a small variety of objects, create prints, then leave the objects next to the tray and ask children to guess which object made certain patterns.

Observation questions

- Do the children know basic shapes?
- Do the children show interest in the characteristics of patterns? Do they notice small details?

Christmas ice world

Shallow trays

What you need:

- Shallow tray
- Aluminium foil
- Ice cubes
- Pine tree branches
- Green paper
- Colouring pens, glitter, sequins
- Scissors
- Plastic figures or pebbles

What's in it for the children?

Children will be able to grasp the characteristics of a season through seasonal small world provocations. They can learn about traditions and customs whilst also having fun. The frame of the small world provides them with time and freedom to process new information at their own pace.

Taking it forward

- For a sensory play effect, add coloured ice cubes, red glitter and scented oil.

Observation questions

- Do the children visualise stories from their life?
- Do the children talk while playing?

What to do:

1. Discuss the scene that will be set.
2. Place a shallow tray safely on a stand, table or on the ground.
3. Cover the bottom of the tray with aluminium foil.
4. Decorate the sides with pine tree branches and add ice cubes.
5. Make a simple paper Christmas tree: cut a disc out of the green paper - the bigger the circle, the taller the tree. The children can then decorate the disc with glitter, sequins etc. Once they're finished and the decoration has dried, cut a small triangle wedge out of the disc and bring the sides of the cut together to form a cone. Tape the cone closed and prop it up for your own miniature Christmas tree.
6. Make pebble people by drawing on flat pebbles. Alternatively, add play figures.
7. Work alongside the children as they play and encourage them to act out winter/Christmas related stories and nursery rhymes.

Native American reserve

Shallow trays

What you need:

- Shallow tray
- Twigs
- Cardboard
- Coloured felt fabric
- Coloured paper
- Twine
- Scissors
- White paper and pencil
- Glue
- Soil
- Fresh grass or moss
- Stones or sand
- Pebbles
- Orange tissue paper or wool
- Native American play figures

What to do:

1. Discuss the scene that will be set, looking at pictures of native American lifestyle.
2. To make the tepee: for the base of the teepee, trace a circle roughly 10 cm in diameter. Mark out and gently puncture five evenly spaced holes around the base circle, leaving a wide gap between two holes as the teepee's entrance. Next, select five evenly sized twigs. Glue the twigs vertically into the holes and bring them together to meet in the centre of the base, tying them together with twine. You may need add more glue and twine before the base is stable. You can now cut out your felt teepee canvas (you can practice with paper first, and adjust your measurements accordingly). Drape the canvas around teepee, and secure either with twine, knots or the glue.
3. Place a shallow tray safely on a stand, table or on the ground.
4. Cover the bottom of the tray half with grass, half with stones or sand Add a curly blue paper strip to represent a river.
5. Create a fire by making a circle of pebbles and adding orange paper strips or orange wool.
7. Add twigs, tepees and play people.
8. Work alongside the children as they play and encourage them to act out stories.

What's in it for the children?

Children will be able to focus on various cultural aspects, including the meaning of different tribes, colour, shape and animal symbolism, and general beliefs. This will widen their knowledge and interest about the world.

Taking it forward

- Make a variety of tribal cultural scenes such as African, South-American etc.

Observation questions

- Can the children manipulate the scene in order to achieve their play aims?
- Can the children empathise with different lifestyles?

Bath time

Shallow trays

What you need:

- Shallow tray
- Bubble bath
- Sponge pieces
- Fabric pieces
- Small dolls or other play people

What to do:

1. Place a shallow tray safely on a stand, table or on the ground.
2. Fill it with water and bubble bath.
3. Add small dolls or play figures and provide pieces of sponge and fabric as face/wash cloths.
4. Encourage the children to bathe the play people and name their body parts.
5. Sing related nursery rhymes such as 'Heads, shoulders, knees and toes', 'The hokey cokey', 'Tommy Thumb' whilst pointing out the body parts on the dolls.

Taking it forward

- Name body parts in different languages.

Observation questions

- Do the children display self-awareness?
- Are the children confidently talking about themselves and their bodies?

What's in it for the children?

Children will have fun with the water and the bubbles, whilst deepening their knowledge about their own bodies. They will also have the opportunity to being caring instead of being cared for.

The Easter egg hunt

Shallow trays

What you need:

- Shallow tray
- Real grass or green tissue paper
- Real flowers
- Paper
- Pencils and crayons
- Clay or playdough
- Tweezers
- Tongs
- Wooden pegs
- Chopsticks

What to do:

1. Discuss the scene that will be set, including old traditions at Easter.
2. Create Easter eggs with the children from paper, clay or playdough. Let them explore the different materials and decorate their eggs as they wish
3. Place a shallow tray safely on a stand, table or on the ground.
4. Fill the tray with cut up green tissue paper or real grass and scatter real flowers on the top.
5. Hide the children's Easter egg creations underneath.
6. Provide children with a variety of picking objects, tweezers, tongs, wooden pegs, chopsticks etc., and encourage them to find the eggs using only the tools provided.
7. Work alongside the children as they play and explain that some people and animals have restricted abilities and use equipment to help them.
8. Discuss the experience with the children.

What's in it for the children?

Through this play scene children will gain new perspectives about people and the world around them. The opportunity to experience the feeling of being restricted will aid children in appreciating their own abilities and in respecting the differences of others in their environment.

Taking it forward

- Make a bird feeding station and practise the picking skills of birds
- Hide miniature objects under the grass with a small part of the objects remaining visible and play 'I spy' game, asking the children to guess what they see

Observation questions

- Can the children notice differences between living beings?
- Do the children accept and respect differences?

Creepy crawlies

Water worlds

What you need:

- Water tray
- Soil and water
- Coffee beans to represent the swamp (optional)
- Stones and rocks
- Log and bark pieces
- Real plants (optional)
- Toy creepy crawlies

What to do:

1. Discuss the scene that will be set and ask the children to plan their ideas.
2. Place the water tray safely on a stand, table or on the ground.
3. Cover the bottom of the tray with some soil, then pour a little water over it.
4. Place coffee beans in one corner to represent a swamp area.
5. Add rocks, stones, tree bark pieces and plants, then add the creepy crawlies.
6. Work alongside the children as they play and encourage them to act out stories and talk about the characteristics of the animals.

What's in it for the children?

Through this small world play activity the children will be using different senses. They will be exploring, observing, making associations from previous experiences and attempting to cognitively map the new knowledge with their previous understanding.

Taking it forward

- Make a fairy swamp pet station by adding glitter and using only toy ladybirds.

Observation questions

- Can the children ask questions based on their experiences?
- Do the children bring personal experiences into their play?

Under the sea

Water worlds

What you need:

- Plastic bottle
- Blue food colouring
- 200 ml baby oil
- Small shells and pebbles
- Strong glue or glue gun

What to do:

1. Discuss the scene that will be set and ask the children to plan their ideas.
2. First pour approximately 200 ml of baby oil into the plastic bottle.
3. Drop a variety of shells and pebbles through the neck of the bottle.
4. Stir a very small amount of blue food colouring into some water, then tip it on top of the oil.
5. Talk to the children about what happens to the two liquids when they met each other.
6. Seal the lid securely with strong glue or a glue gun.
7. Tip the bottle from side to side to make some waves and large bubbles. When air is trapped in the oil it creates bubbles which last for longer than those in water. Observe them moving slowly until they pop.

What's in it for the children?

Through this scientific experiment children will have the opportunity to develop a range of skills and knowledge: they will gain an understanding that oil and water do not mix, learning how air can be trapped in liquids, talking about the shape and nature of waves, naming and describing sea creatures and shells, talking about habitats. Their sensory experience will include visual stimulus and colour mixing. They will have the opportunity to invent stories using the bottle as a prop for their imagination.

Taking it forward

- Carry out the investigation in an open tray and discuss the idea of water pollution.

Observation questions

- Are the children focussed and engaged for extended periods of time?
- Do the children show interest in basic level physics?

Mermaid's palace

Water worlds

What you need:

- *The Little Mermaid* storybook
- **Water tray** (ideally transparent, so children can observe what happens under the water)
- **Plastic building bricks**
- **Play figures** (people and animals)
- **Rocks, stones, pebbles, shells and some plants**

What to do:

1. Read *The Little Mermaid* storybook together and talk about the characters in the story.
2. Discuss the scene that will be set and ask the children to plan their ideas.
3. Create the mermaid's palace out of plastic building bricks.
4. Place the water tray safely on a stand, table or on the ground.
5. Place the palace in the middle of the tray then add rocks, stones, pebbles, shells and some plants for a realistic effect.
6. Fill up with water, then observe how water changes the scene.
7. Work alongside the children as they play and encourage them to retell the story of *The Little Mermaid*.

What's in it for the children?

Children can observe how water changes perspective and, therefore gain a basic understanding of physical characteristics and rules such as density, weight, floating/sinking etc.

Taking it forward

- Organise a small world featuring different elements such as building a high structure for 'Jack and the Beanstalk' to understand height, using a fan to represent the wolf's huff and puff in 'Three Little Pigs' etc.

Observation questions

- Do the children display curiosity about discovering?
- Do the children show interest in changes within their environment?

Pirate ship

Water worlds

What you need:

- Water tray
- Blue gravel stones or beads
- Rice or shredded coconut soaked in blue food colouring
- Coins
- Costume jewellery
- Twigs or driftwood sticks
- String or strong thread
- Pirate play figures

What to do:

1. Discuss the scene that will be set and ask the children to plan their ideas.
2. Make a twig boat or raft: weave together the twigs. The best way to do this is for the adult to hold the twigs in line, and the child to wrap the string around them. Tie the string at one end of the first twig and then weave it over and under the rest of the twigs in the line. Repeat this back and forth in both directions until the ship/raft is holding together firmly.
3. Place the water tray safely on a stand, table or on the ground.
4. Put blue beads or gravel, jewellery and coins on the bottom.
5. Add rocks, stones and pebbles for a realistic effect.
6. Fill up the tray with water, then add the boat and pirate figures.
7. Work alongside the children as they play and encourage them to act out stories and talk about their experiences.

What's in it for the children?

Children can role play and act out various experiences they may have had, or something that is of some interest to them.

Taking it forward

- Make a large scene with connecting water trays. Prepare a treasure map and follow the route with the figures.
- Record the children's stories for a movie afternoon.

Observation questions

- Can the children ask questions based on their experiences?
- Do the children bring personal experiences into their play?

Floating structures

Water worlds

What you need:

- Water tray
- Polystyrene pieces
- Small, light building bricks

What to do:

1. Place the water tray safely on a stand, table or on the ground.
2. Break up a piece of polystyrene foam into palm sized pieces, and place them on the water.
3. Work alongside the children as they play and encourage them to build structures on the polystyrene pieces (platforms).
4. In the meantime, comment on the experiments with specific vocabulary such as: too long, too wide, wobbly, sturdy etc.

What's in it for the children?

During this activity children can experiment with some basic rules of physics and the unique characteristics of things such as weight or capacity. This early experience helps children to develop an interest in the world around them that will further trigger their curiosity and need to find out.

Taking it forward

- Create a variety of floating building platforms using plastic egg boxes, plastic box lids, sponge, flat wooden block/disc etc.
- Organise a themed variation such as 'the big arctic swim' (place plastic arctic animal toys on the polystyrene pieces) or 'the pirate move' (collect a variety of jewellery items, place them on the polystyrene pieces and try to move them on the water surface from one end to the other).

Observation questions

- Do the children notice differences and changes?
- Do the children engage with science experiments? Do they have ideas?

Fishing trip

Water worlds

What you need:

- **Water tray**
- **Art foam**
- **Wire**
- **Piece of leather**
- **Net pack** (the kind that hold fruit etc.)
- **Needle and thread**
- **Long, strong stick**
- **String**
- **Paper clips**
- **Rocks, stones, shells, water plants** (optional)

What to do:

1. Discuss the scene that will be set and ask the children to plan their ideas.
2. Cut out mini fish from art foam.
3. Make a fishing net: twist the wire in to a hoop with a handle, then glue the leather to the handle to create a grip. Place the net bag in the hoop, fold the top of the net over the hoop, and sew it in place.
4. Make a fishing rod: tie string to the thinner end of a long, strong stick. Fold out a paper clip, secure one side to the string and form a hook from the other end.
5. Place the water tray safely on a stand, table or on the ground.
6. Add rocks, stones, pebbles, shells and some plants for a realistic effect.
7. Fill the tray up with water, then add in the foam fish.
8. Work alongside the children as they play and encourage them to catch the fish.

What's in it for the children?

With this activity, children can get engaged with both imaginative and physical play. Their hand-eye coordination and fine motor skills will develop whilst trying to catch the fish, but they can also express their creative thoughts by telling the story of a fishing trip.

Taking it forward

- Create a magnetic fishing game for smaller children: place a piece of curled wire on the front of the foam fish, then secure a small magnet on the end of the string fishing line instead of a hook.

Observation questions

- Can the children concentrate on small tasks?
- Do the children engage in the creation of small world?

Rainy play

Water worlds

What you need:

- Water tray
- On old, possibly transparent umbrella with a curled handle
- Ribbon
- Sharp knife or scissors
- Variety of containers, cups and jugs

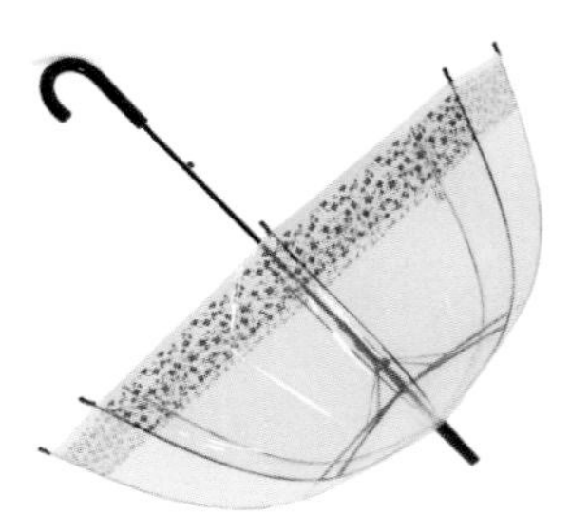

What to do:

1. Discuss the children's experience of rain, then introduce the theme of the scene that will be set.
2. Place the water tray safely on a stand, table or on the ground and fill with some water.
3. Poke holes into the top of the umbrella, not too big and not too many, so that it lets water out very slowly when filled.
4. Tie a ribbon on the curled handle of the umbrella and secure it above the water tray (do not use lamps or utility pipes for this purpose), so the umbrella is upside down.
5. Pour some water into the umbrella.
6. Encourage the children to collect the falling water.
7. Sing and act out rain-related nursery rhymes, such as 'Rain, rain go away', 'I hear thunder', 'Incy Wincy Spider' and so on.

What's in it for the children?

Playing in unusual circumstances will strengthen children's ability to positively respond to unknown and/or difficult situations. The changes in the environment entertain and inspire children, and highlights for them their own ability to adapt and embrace new things in their lives.

Taking it forward

- Create a scene for 'The Wise Man built his house' ... song by forming a sand and a rock hill, then observe the effect of the falling water on both. See the activity 'House on the rocks' on page 17.

Observation questions

- Can the children play comfortably in unusual circumstances?
- Do the children respond to change?

Snakes

Water worlds

What you need:

- Transparent water tray
- Light table, or some outdoor fairy lights and tape
- Water beads
- Rocks
- Water plants
- Toy snakes and other creepy crawlies, or snakes made from aluminium foil

What to do:

1. Soak the water beads in water overnight, following the packet instructions.
2. Place the water tray safely on the light table or tape some waterproof, outdoor fairy lights on the bottom of the water tray.
3. Switch the light table or the lights on and darken the room.
4. Place the inflated water beads in the bottom of the tray and add decorative features such as rocks and plants.
5. Place in the creepy crawly toys.
6. Work alongside the children as they play and encourage them to build stories and create characters.

What's in it for the children?

Children will benefit from opportunities to explore light properly when the surrounding environment is dark. Light boxes add interest to any setting, creating a place for careful observation or for discovering pattern, shape, form, colour, opacity and colour mixing. The calming influence of light and dark invites sensory exploration and engages children's attention for long periods of time. By their nature, the materials that are used to explore light promote aesthetic awareness and an appreciation of appearance.

Taking it forward

- Use torches to observe the features and details of the creatures.
- Change the colour of the light and observe different perspectives

Observation questions

- How do children react to changes in the environment?
- Do they recall memories and experiences in response to the environment?

Swamp

Water worlds

What you need:

- **Water tray**
- **Playdough:**
  - **70 g flour**
  - **60 g cornflour**
  - **3 tbs cocoa powder**
  - **50 g salt**
  - **3 tsp lemon juice**
  - **3 tbsp oil**
  - **110 ml boiling water**
- **Broccoli** (or other dark green vegetables)
- **Fresh flowers**
- **Rocks**
- **Earth**
- **Swamp animal toys** (turtle, alligator, fish, frog)

What to do:

1. Make the playdough by mixing all the ingredients together to form a brown dough.
2. Place the water tray safely on a stand, table or on the ground.
3. Pour some water into it (make it very shallow).
4. Add features: balls of brown playdough, earth, rocks, broccoli florets.
5. Finally, place in the animals.
6. Work alongside the children as they play and encourage them to build stories and create characters.

What's in it for the children?

A small world scene and the related imaginative play is a great, safe frame for children to explore, discover their world or to process and test newly gained knowledge. When playing with scenes that involve adverse opinions (something being yucky, disgusting, scary etc.), children can develop their own feelings and viewpoints.

Taking it forward

- Add natural elements to create a varied swamp look: coffee beans, popcorn, dry rice, watercress, soapy water, lentils etc.

Observation questions

- Do the children use descriptive language and an extended vocabulary when playing?
- Do the children express ideas?

Jelly spy

Sand tray

What you need:

- Water tray
- Jelly cubes or gelatine
- Very small real and toy objects

What to do:

1. Make the jelly the day before the play is planned, following the instructions on the packet. If using gelatine sheets/powder, add some food colouring too.
2. Place the water tray safely on a stand or on the ground and fill with the jelly.
3. Hide the small objects under the jelly.
4. Encourage the children to use various senses to detect the objects. For example: blindfold the children and encourage them to find objects by touch, or ask a designated child to choose and describe an object (by colour, size or other characteristics) for the other children to identify the object in the jelly.
5. Organise competitions to see who finds the most objects.

What's in it for the children?

Small world scenes provide a great framework for many types of sensory play. This activity, through the senses of smell, vision and touch, uses and inspires multiple reactions in the body. The sensory experiences help to stimulate the brain by sending signals that will strengthen neural pathways, being important for all types of learning.

Taking it forward

- Create scenes with other medium such as dry rice, flour or lentils to hide the toys..

Observation questions

- Do the children use a variety of senses naturally?
- Do the children respond to sensory stimulation?

Big city

Cereal box play

What you need:

- Cereal box or a flatter, oblong box
- Pictures of London or another big city
- Cardboard rolls
- White card
- Markers
- Double sided tape
- Sticky tape

What to do:

1. Take off one large side of the cereal box or flatter oblong box to create a small tray.
2. Draw simple line drawings/silhouettes or outlines of iconic buildings/attractions from London or another famous big city.
3. Cut around them and secure cardboard rolls on the back as standing support.
4. Draw simple roads going around the box using a marker.
5. Look at pictures of London or another city and arrange the landmarks similarly to the real city layout.
6. Introduce toy features such as people or cars to the scene.
7. Work alongside the children as they play and encourage them to personalise the scene, possibly using their own memories, or photographs they have of big cities.

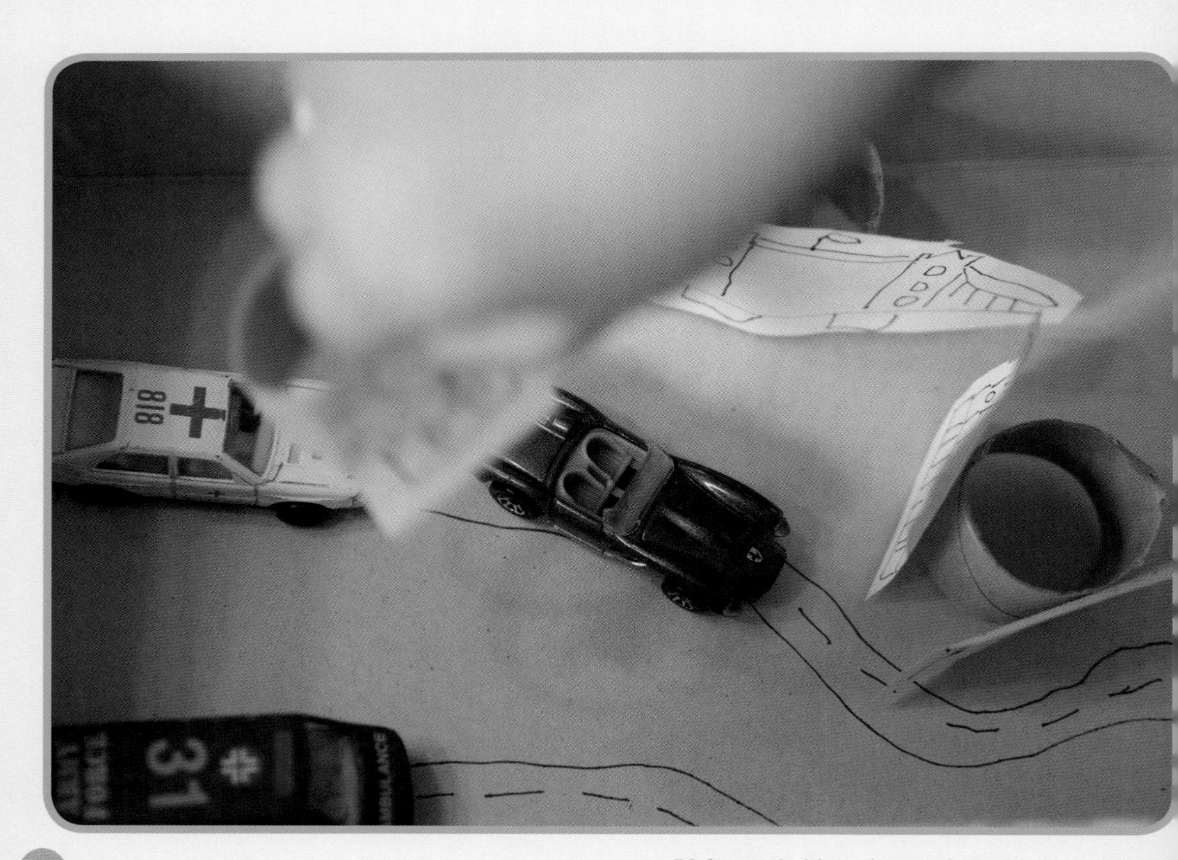

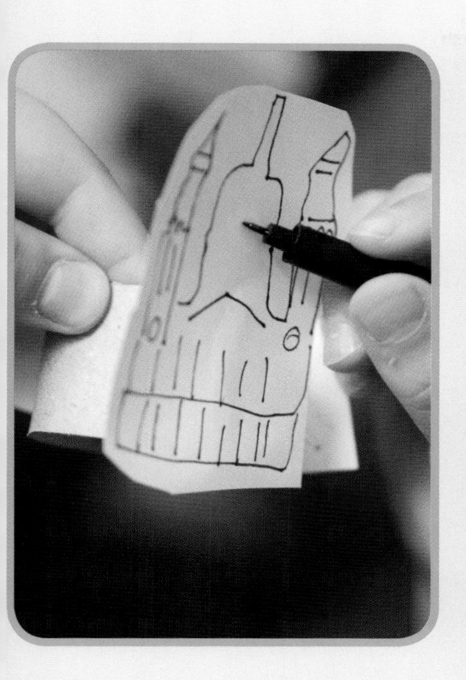

What's in it for the children?

Experimenting with materials reformed and reconstructed for a scene will result in sustained concentration, and in both independent play and co-operation. Children will use their knowledge and ideas to manipulate objects and complete processes, which will aid the development of their thinking skills.

Taking it forward

- Collect a wide range of empty boxes and encourage the children to make a city skyline by stacking them side by side. Use paints and craft materials to decorate.
- Use building bricks to make group constructions, encouraging the children to work together.

Observation questions

- Do the children show an interest in their environment?
- Do children understand simple references to real life within their play?

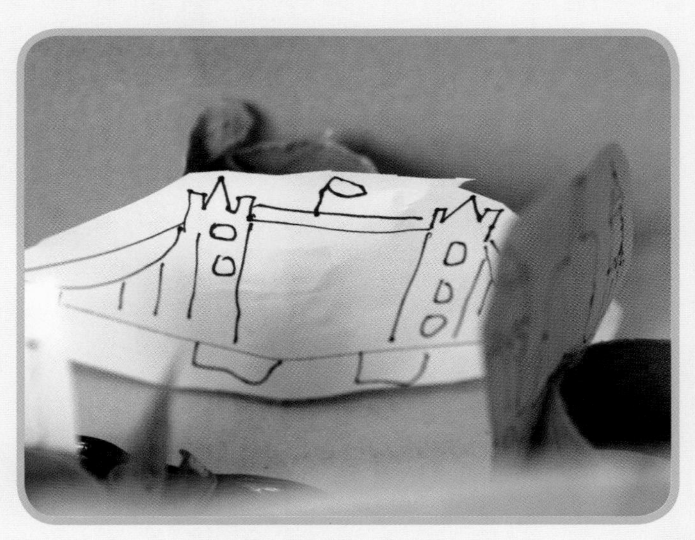

Animal wonderland

Cereal box play

What you need:

- Cereal box
- Lentils/rice/sesame seeds/ linseeds
- Bag of flour
- Silver glitter
- Cotton wool balls
- Pine cones
- Glass beads or white stones
- Animal figures

What to do:

1. Discuss the life of animals in the winter.
2. Take off one large side of the cereal box to create a small tray.
3. Place small circles of the seeds in various places on the bottom.
4. Cover fully with flour.
5. Place the decorative items around the box to create the landscape.
6. Introduce the animals to the scene and encourage the children to act out the animals looking for food.
7. Work alongside the children as they play and encourage them to wonder about questions like how animals find food in the winter.

What's in it for the children?

This small world scene helps children to understand the variety of living creatures on Earth. The knowledge gained through different play scenes will be represented in children's future decisions about how to approach their own environment and how to find their own place in the world.

Taking it forward

- Provide the children with a variety of tools to look for food as an animal would (such as tongs for the spoonbill, tweezers for birds, wire grabber tool for elephant , chopsticks for stork etc).

Observation questions

- Do the children show empathy towards other living things?
- Can children operate small tools?

Train track

Cereal box play

What you need:

- Cereal box
- Felt tip pens
- Small train toys
- Blocks to build the scene
- Decorative items to create trees, hills etc.
- Play people

What to do:

1. Take off one large side of the cereal box to create a small tray.
2. Draw a simple train track going around the box using a marker.
3. Leave some markers for the children to add anything extra to the scene that they want.
4. Encourage children to build the landscape from small building blocks and to place the decorative items around the box to complete the landscape.
5. Introduce toy trains and people to the scene.
6. Work alongside the children as they play and encourage them to personalise the scene.

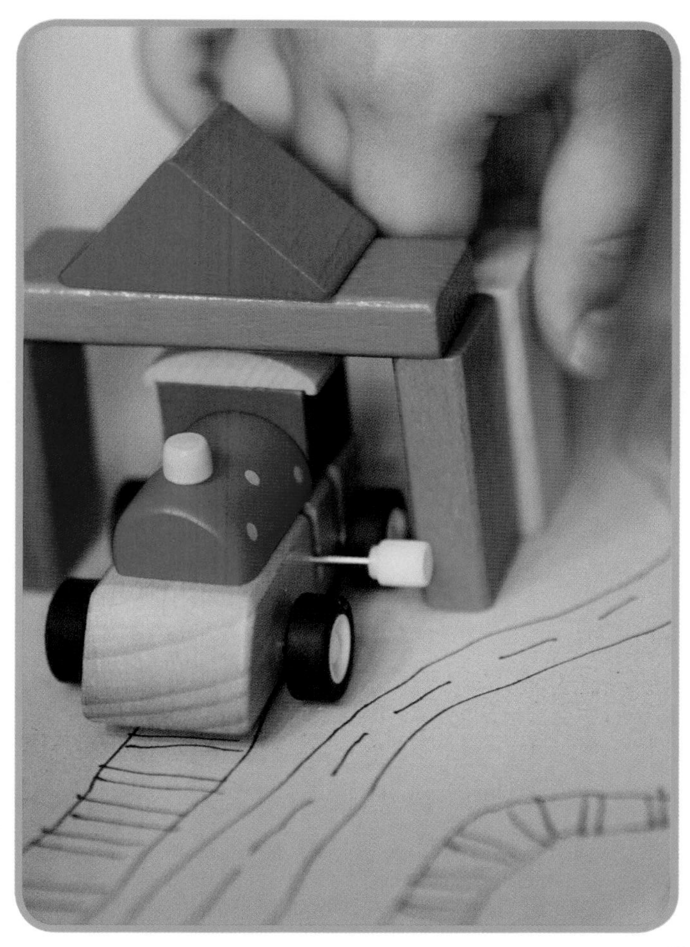

What's in it for the children?

This small world scene develops knowledge and understanding through construction of real world transport/ road systems. It develops literacy through labelling objects and mark making. Building with solid shapes, counting, manipulating objects, sorting and matching will advance children's understanding of mathematical concepts. It will help children's physical development, in particular their fine motor skills, co-ordination and gross motor abilities through stacking and balancing.

Taking it forward

- Use a large box so children can sit/ move in the scene.
- Act out train related stories such as 'Thomas the Tank Engine'.

Observation questions

- Do the children call on real life experiences when creating a play scene?
- Can children use a variety of skills to achieve a final goal?

Tunnels and roads

Cereal box play

What you need:

- Cereal box
- Marker and felt tip pens
- Cardboard rolls and paper towel tubes
- Small toy cars
- Scissors/craft knife
- Double-sided tape
- Sticky tape

What to do:

1. Take off one large side of the cereal box to create a small tray.
2. Draw simple roads going around the box using a marker.
3. Cut the paper rolls with a craft knife lengthwise or encourage children to cut smaller rolls with scissors.
4. Encourage children to draw/build the landscape using markers, the paper rolls and tape.
5. Introduce toy cars to the scene.
6. Work alongside the children as they play and encourage them to personalise the scene.
7. Alternatively cut the large side of the box, then turn it upside down, draw roads on the top and cut little tunnel entrances (small semi-circles) on the side, so two-level traffic is achieved.

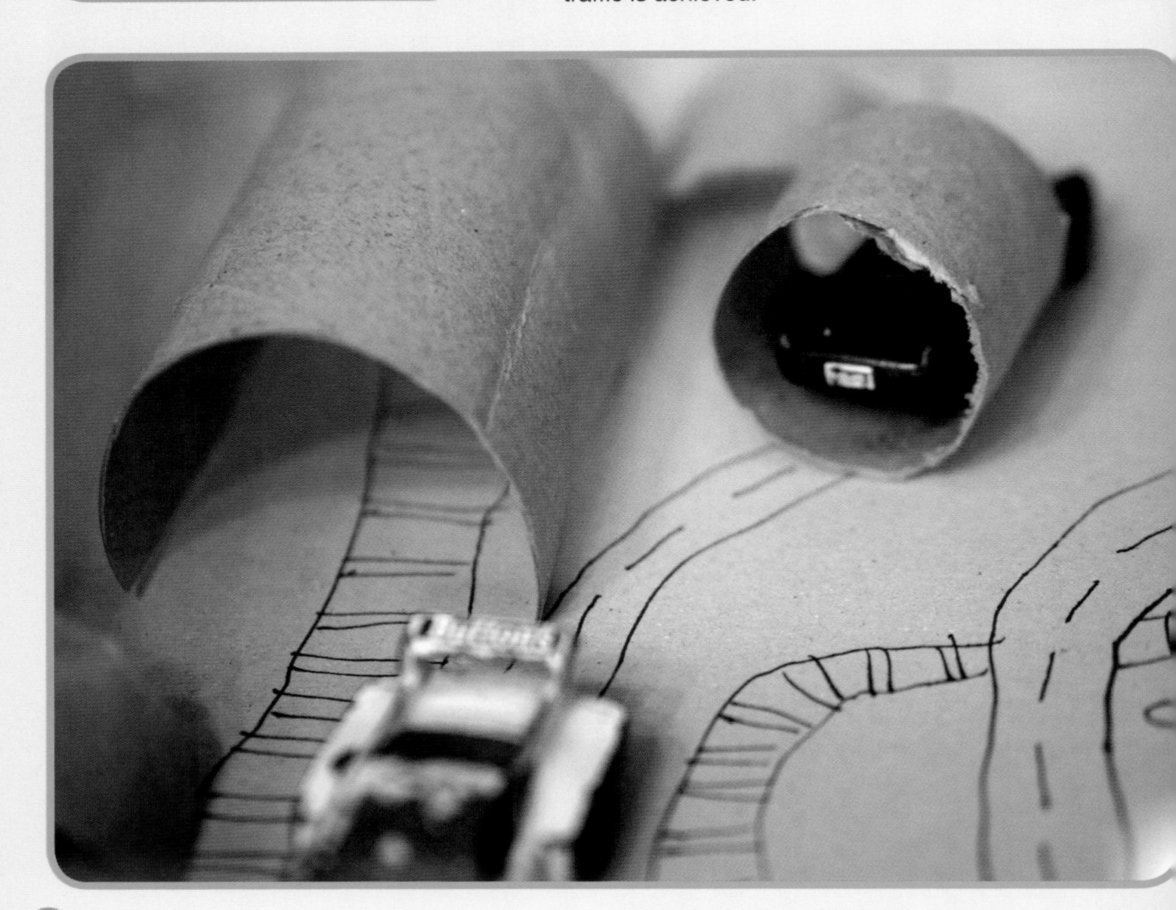

What's in it for the children?

Experimenting with materials reformed and reconstructed for a scene will result in sustained concentration, and in both independent play and co-operation. Children will use their knowledge and ideas to manipulate objects and complete processes, which will aid the development of their thinking skills.

Taking it forward

- Build a child-sized tunnel system from cardboard boxes.
- Make a 'natural tunnels and roads' small world, using bark shells etc.

Observation questions

- Do the children make and execute plans?
- Can the children demonstrate forward thinking to work on more complex play projects?

Magic forest

Cereal box play

What you need:

- Cereal box
- Sticks, moss, log and bark pieces
- Twine
- Houseleek (sempervivum)
- Small yoghurt pots
- Earth and gravel
- Thin wire
- Clay
- Glitter, feathers
- Fairy play figures

What's in it for the children?

This small world scene fosters creativity through imaginative play, using props and real objects, creating characters and taking on a role. It strengthens literacy through oral storytelling by using storybook language when inventing stories. It also develops knowledge and understanding of the world through planting and caring for plants and understanding what plants need to survive.

Taking it forward

- Children can create their own fairies by drawing faces on, then cutting and sticking wings onto clothes pegs.
- Create clay fairy furniture.

Observation questions

- Do the children have an understanding of time (such as how often to water the plants, how long it lives etc.)?
- Do the children invent stories?

What to do:

1. Discuss the scene that will be set and ask the children to plan their ideas.
2. Take off one large side of the cereal box to create a small tray.
3. Cover the bottom of the box with moss and feathers.
4. Place log and bark pieces scattered around.
5. To make a fairy washing line: cut a length of wire, wrap one end around the top of a stick, then repeat it on the other side. Secure into the ground and hang fairy leaf-clothes on it.
6. To make a decorative clay mushroom: mould a small piece of clay into a shape that resembles a shallow cup, roll a piece for the stem of the mushroom (a medium sized cylindrical shape with rounded edges), then attach them to each other with a little water.
7. Plant houseleeks in tiny yoghurt pots: make small holes into the bottom of the pot, place a thin layer of gravel inside, fill the rest up with earth and plant the houseleek.
8. Work alongside the children as they play and encourage them to act out stories and talk about the characteristics of their fairies.
9. The fairy garden can be left, looked after and played with for longer periods of time.

Car wash

Cereal box play

What you need:

- Small cardboard box
- Craft knife
- Paint
- Bubble wrap
- Felt
- Wooden rods
- Paper towel tubes
- Paper
- Hot glue gun

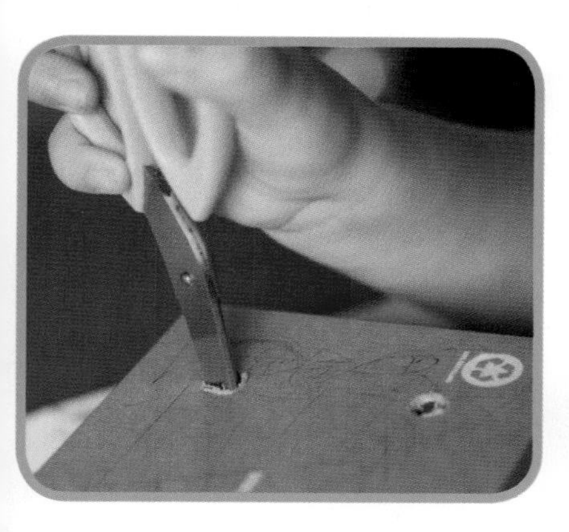

What's in it for the children?

Children will use their knowledge and ideas to manipulate objects and complete processes, which will aid the development of their thinking skills.

Taking it forward

- Build a system of car wash buildings and separate them by car type (trucks, tractors, vans etc). Appoint leaders for each car wash and take it in turns.

Observation questions

- Do the children use their imaginations when playing?
- Can the children share and work together?

What to do:

1. Cut off the top of the cardboard box as well as the entrance door and the exit. Leaving the car wash without a ceiling means the children can move the cars inside and see how the brushes wash their cars.
2. Paint the outside of the box to protect the cardboard from getting wet to some extent.
3. Protect the inside by gluing bubble wrap on the two main walls and the floor.
4. Create the horizontal brushes: cut the wooden rods to the desired length. Use a craft knife to cut holes in the cardboard on both sides and insert the rods. Cut the felt for the brushes and glue onto the rods using a hot glue gun.
5. Cut the felt for the exit streamers and glue it on the inside.
6. Create the vertical brushes: cut felt and glue it to paper towel tubes. Glue these to the cardboard just before the exit opening.
7. Write the words 'Car Wash Entrance' and 'Exit' on paper. Cut the letters out and glue them at the entrance and exit.

Speckled Frogs

Cereal box play

What you need:

- Cereal box
- Blue and green card or fabric material such as felt or silk
- Wood pieces, twigs etc.
- Glass beads, pebbles
- Frog toy figures (alternatively ask children to draw frogs)
- Books about frog life

What to do:

1. Cut off one side of the cereal box to create a shallow tray.
2. Place green card on the bottom, then cut a rough blue circle for the pond.
3. Scatter around green felt leaves and glass pebbles.
4. Cut felt or card lily-pads.
5. Place the tree/wood pieces on the 'shore' of the pond.
6. Support children's learning with books about the frog life-cycle, and count and sing *Five little speckled frogs* with them.

What's in it for the children?

Combining science, story-telling, non-fiction information books, singing, music making and numeracy play, this is a versatile small world activity area to set up. Children can sing songs, recite text from memory, count, creativity, create sounds using everyday objects and materials, make music to accompany songs, create animal and nature sounds whilst also learning about life-cycles and animal habitats based on their understanding of non-fiction books.

Taking it forward

- Provide natural materials (sticks, bags of pebbles, shells etc.) to create music for the nursery rhyme.
- Add aqua beads/water beads to represent frogspawn and demonstrate their life-cycle.

Observation questions

- Do the children use basic mathematic skills?
- Are the children interested in simple science?

Waterfall

Cereal box play

What you need:

- Two cereal boxes
- Blue card
- Long blue fabric
- Fairy lights
- Double-sided tape
- Real plants in pots
- Drift wood or other wood pieces
- Pebbles
- Toy pond animals

What to do:

1. Cut off the large side of two cardboard boxes to create shallow trays.
2. Cut and place a piece of blue card into the bottom of both boxes.
3. Place one tray on a table, the other one on the floor next to the table.
4. Place and secure one end of the fabric under the top tray.
5. Arrange the plants, decorative wooden items and pebbles on the top tray.
6. Take the other end of the fabric and place it in the bottom tray in a draping, flowing style.
7. Place and secure a stream of fairy lights on the draped fabric (to represent flowing water).
8. Arrange decorative pond items in the bottom tray.
9. Encourage the children to create and act out factual or fiction stories.

What's in it for the children?

Symbolic play is the ability of children to use objects, actions or ideas to represent other objects, actions, or ideas as play. Small world play enhances the child's ability for make-believe play by providing loose parts that have more than one purpose, such as wooden pieces, small pebbles and non-realistic materials that can be imagined symbolically as other objects.

Taking it forward

- Introduce small paper boats to the scene.
- Replace the trays with plastic trays and the fabric with guttering and introduce water to the scene in bottles and watering cans for experimentation.

Observation questions

- Do the children mix a variety of expression forms such as movement, singing, talking etc. to create a play scene?

Billy Goats Gruff

Cereal box play

What you need:

- Cereal box
- Blue and brown card
- Clay in different colours
- Feathers
- Wood chippings
- Three goat toy figures
- Fresh grass

What to do:

1. Cut off a large side of the cereal box so to create a shallow tray.
2. Cover the bottom of the box tray with blue card to represent water.
3. Cut a strip of brown card and secure it to two opposite sides of the tray to create an arched bridge.
4. Make clay trolls: preferably use pale yellow, brown and black clay. Form a troll head by rolling a ball and pinching two large ears on either side. Create a troll body by rolling a cylinder and pinching clumsy limbs. Attach the head to the body using water to blend and make hair from yarn. Decorate with feather and wood chippings.
5. Place the fresh grass on one side and the goats on the other.
6. Encourage the children to act out variations of the original 'Billy Goat Gruff' story, asking questions such as 'What if ...'.

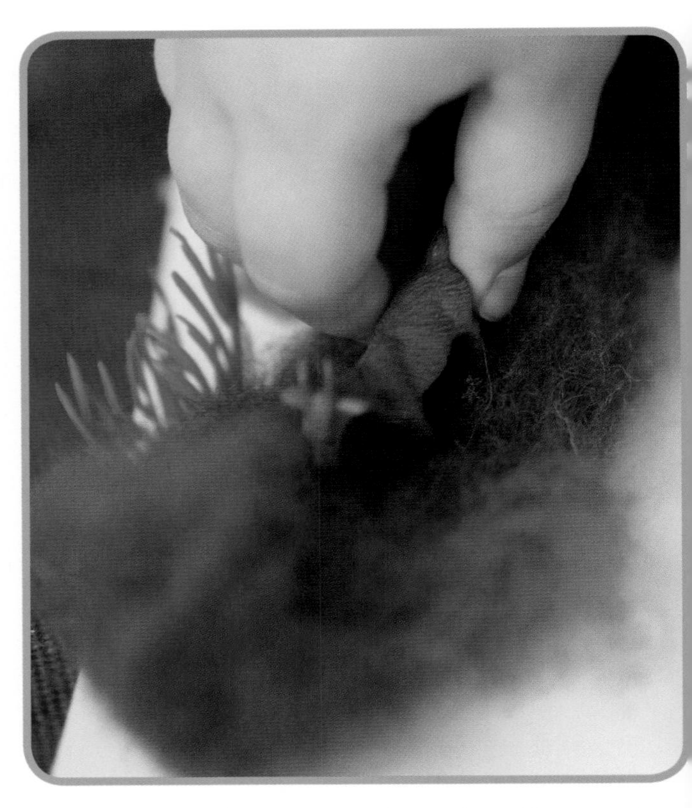

What's in it for the children?

Understanding a story through the experiences of a character enables children to feel what it could have been like to be someone else. Stories help children to consider the impact of events, significant or otherwise, in the life of animals or ordinary people.

Taking it forward

- Use a very large cardboard box to create a life-sized scene for the children to act out the roles themselves.

Observation questions

- Can the children pretend to be someone else?
- Do the children express feelings/ empathy with regards to others?

The Gruffalo

Cereal box play

What you need:

- Cereal box
- Clay
- Matchsticks
- Pine cones , acorns
- Real leaves
- Air-dying clay (optional)
- A green pom pom
- Googly eyes
- White and silver pipe cleaners
- Purple craft foam cut into triangles
- Cookie cutter letters
- Toy snake, owl, mouse
- Storybook *The Gruffalo* by Julia Donaldson

What to do:

1. Read the story of 'The Gruffalo' together.
2. Cut off the large side of the box to create a tray.
3. Cover the bottom of the tray with clay, pressing with fingers.
4. Push matchsticks into certain areas to represent the forest.
5. Scatter around pine cones, acorns and real leaves.
6. Make a clay Gruffalo: roll two big balls, four medium cylinders and two small balls from clay. Form the Gruffalo's head and body from the big balls, attach these to each other. Attach the limbs and finally form two ears from the small balls. Make nails from silver pipe cleaners and use the white pipe cleaners to make whiskers, tusks and horns. Finally add eyes, green nose and purple foam prickles.
7. Place the toy figures within the small world scene and encourage the children to recite and act out the story.

What's in it for the children?

Experimenting with materials reformed and reconstructed for a scene will result in sustained concentration, and in both independent play and co-operation. Children will use knowledge and ideas to manipulate objects and complete processes, which will aid the development of their thinking skills.

Taking it forward

- Create the Gruffalo's forest for the different seasons and add seasonal touches.
- Create a small world scene based on the storybook *The Gruffalo's Child*.

Observation questions

- Are the children able to recall a storyline?
- Do the children engage with changing roles?

Chinese New Year

Freeform small worlds

What you need:

- Small suitcase
- Plates/small bowls from a doll house set
- Bag of dry rice
- Tweezers and/or chopsticks
- Small serving spoons
- Chinese labels
- Red marker, red paper

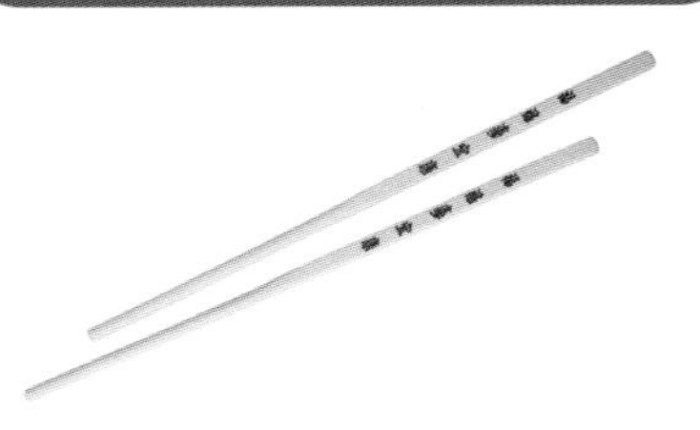

What's in it for the children?

Celebrating diversity can be done in a whole range of ways such as through objects, texts and photographs, showing young children that people and cultures all over the world are very different, and through reading story books that highlight that many countries have culturally diverse societies. Celebrating religious and cultural events will bring excitement and variety in the daily activities of children who will in turn embrace and not fear difference.

Taking it forward

- Prepare different festival small world sets such as Diwali, Eid etc.
- Aid children in preparing their individual Chinese small world sets.

Observation questions

- Are the children interested in other cultures?
- Do the children show interest in different types of texts?
- Can the children differentiate colours?

What to do:

1. Talk to children about Chinese New Year customs.
2. Look at pictures and Chinese money, letters and texts.
3. Prepare the suitcase, by placing in a bag of rice, small plates/bowls, tweezers or chopsticks.
4. Chopsticks can be replaced by sticks collected by the children.
5. Place in red items and tell children that red symbolises the act of chasing evil spirits away.
6. Print out images of Chinese money and talk about the tradition of Chinese children receiving red envelopes full of money (instead of wrapped gifts that other nationalities give at Christmas). Explain that the amount they receive is usually an even number but the amount cannot be divisible by four, because in Chinese beliefs the number four means death.
7. Encourage children to use the utensils to serve rice.

Tiny Tim

Freeform small worlds

What you need:

- Blue card or fabric representing the bath
- Small plastic cup
- Pieces of sponge
- Bubble blower
- Small soap bars
- Turtle toy

What's in it for the children?

Classic nursery rhymes teach the children about basic life events. Nursery rhymes are a great way to learn early phonic skills, give children practice in pitch and volume as well as in language rhythm (like how the voice sounds when asking a question or when retelling). Nursery rhymes take children to an imaginary world, developing their visualisation skills through the use of actions. Nursery rhymes help children to follow a clear sequence of events.

Taking it forward

- Give Tiny Tim a sensory bath by adding food colouring, glitter and lavender oil to the bath.
- Discuss and study where turtles really live.

Observation questions

- Do the children engage with changing roles? Can the children blow bubbles? Is their muscle control developed?
- Can children understand fiction and jokes?

> **I had a little turtle!**
> *I had a little Turtle, His name was Tiny Tim,*
> *I put him in the bathtub, to see if he could swim.*
> *He drank up all the water and ate a bar of soap.*
> *And now he's got a bubble stuck in his throat.*
> *Bubble, Bubble, Bubble, Bubble, Bubble, Bubble,*
> *Bubble, Bubble, Bubble, Bubble, POP!*

What to do:

1. Teach the children the 'Tiny Tim' nursery rhyme.
2. Set up Tiny Tim's bath and act out the song.
3. Ask questions like 'Why did Tim need a bath?', 'What should Tim have eaten instead of soap?', 'What would happen if you ate soap?' etc.
4. Use the set in water play to add another dimension to the activity.

Campsite

Freeform small worlds

What you need:

- Newspaper for base
- Pebbles
- Woodchipping or sawdust
- Wood pieces
- Coloured fabric (including green)
- Dried flowers
- Two small forked and one straight stick
- Two plastic bottle lids
- Toy people
- Red, yellow and orange pipe cleaners
- Small sticks
- Small white pompoms or cue tips

What to do:

1. Show the children camping pictures and discuss their experiences of camping.
2. Set up the base of the camp: scatter wood chippings on newspaper. Cut out leaves from green material and arrange it with dried flowers to represent nature.
3. To make the simple tent: poke holes in the middle of the bottle lids and push the forked sticks through them to stand them up. Place the straight stick across on the top of the forked sticks and hang a rectangular piece of fabric over (bent in the middle).
4. To make the fire: create a circle of mini sticks and place bent pipe cleaners in the middle to represent fire. Attach cue tips or small white pompoms on sticks to the camper toy people as marshmallow roasting props.
5. Play alongside the children and encourage them to act out stories and imaginary conversations.

What's in it for the children?

Small worlds that represent real life events can be a great way to help children become familiar with or recall important real events in their lives. They can use small world play as a safe frame to process their feelings, opinions and test their ideas.

Taking it forward

- Create themed campsites such as animal visit or Christmas in the camp with additional materials such as grains, forest animal toys, fresh pine and holly etc.

Observation questions

- Are the children building their own experiences into play scenes?
- Do the children engage with each other's memories whilst playing?

Reflections

Freeform small worlds

What you need:

- A variety of make-up mirrors
- Materials with a reflective surface such as aluminium foil, emergency wrap or silver foil card
- Reflective objects such as metal spoon, glass bauble, small metal bowl, silver tinsel, small metal bucket, old CDs
- Storybook *Snow White and the Seven Dwarfs*

What to do:

1. Lay the reflective sheet on the floor/table.
2. Place the reflective objects around the sheet.
3. Use the mirrors to create reflected images, study the images projected on the objects.
4. Encourage the children to look at their own image on the different surfaces.
5. Remind the children of the traditional story of Snow White and discuss the role of Snow White's stepmother, then study how the different surfaces can change the reflection, how faces look different in all.
6. Use as much natural light as possible to maximise the reflective properties of the mirrors and objects.

What's in it for the children?

Science based small worlds develop thoughts, questions and observation opportunities, and with time children will learn facts and definitions. Hands-on science play, where children can touch and see, opens doors to critical thinking and language skills while also providing fun.

Taking it forward

- Use sources of light and darken the room to enhance the reflected images.
- Set up an art activity by placing a doll/toy on the mirror and asking children to draw its reflection.

Observation questions

- Are the children expressing scientific ideas (such as where the light will go, how reflection is created etc.)?
- Do the children describe their own experience? Are they using a variety of words?

Building site

Freeform small worlds

What you need:

- A bag of dry pasta
- Mini marshmallows
- Coffee beans
- Small construction vehicle toys
- Noisy and picture books about construction

What to do:

1. Set up the building site base by placing pasta and marshmallows on the table.
2. Place the construction vehicles on the side.
3. Encourage the children to build simple structures from pasta and marshmallows.
4. Add heaps of coffee beans as mud.
5. Aid the children's play by reading noisy and picture books about construction.

What's in it for the children?

This small world scene helps children in many areas of development: physical, creative, problem-solving and communication skills will be practiced whilst playing. Children will have to negotiate and agree plans and ideas to create and use the scene together.

Taking it forward

- Provide builder outfits for dressing up.
- Encourage the children to mimic the sound of construction toys.

Observation questions

- Can the children prepare and carry out plans?
- Do the children use problem-solving skills?

Heroes and villains

Freeform small worlds

What you need:

- Grey card as base
- Black card strips
- Matchboxes
- Toy cars
- Toy superheroes
- Superhero cartoon magazines

What to do:

1. Set up the grey card as the base of the town on the table.
2. Place the black card strips one after another to mark the roads.
3. Add matchboxes in different positions to represent houses.
4. If desired, make little houses: tape black construction paper to the matchboxes so that they are completely covered. Draw windows on the buildings with white crayon.
5. Introduce the superhero figures and cars to the mini town.
6. Encourage children to act out scenes, conflicts and practise problem-solving and negotiation skills.

What's in it for the children?

The superhero small world play is an independent and unrestricted way of learning conflict resolution. Children can experience positive feeling and events from the healthy superhero play: understand more about 'the good guys' and 'the bad guys' in life, recognise the difference between typical action-oriented play and aggression, figure out how to deal with play that crosses the line to aggression and practice conflict resolution.

Taking it forward

- Make mini superhero peg dolls with the children.

Observation questions

- Can the children display self-control?
- Do the children have ideas about how to solve problems?

Baa Baa Black Sheep

Freeform small worlds

What you need:

- Sheep figures
- Figures of a boy, lady and man
- Cotton wool
- Black marker

Taking it forward

- Make wool-product (to represent what wool can be used for): create simple winter hats for the figures by rolling the cotton wool into long sausages and adding it to a paper cone as fur trimming and pompoms.
- Try to colour the cotton wool with different techniques: soak it in beetroot juice, simply paint or rub in food colouring etc.

Observation questions

- Can the children match numerals and group of objects?
- Do the children understand the notion of paying?

What to do:

1. Create a natural area on the table with pebbles/grass/earth.
2. Set up the sheep, using different colours for varied appearances.
3. Make small balls of the cotton wool to represent the wool and place them around the sheep.
4. Introduce the people figures to the scene and act out the events of 'Baa Baa Black Sheep' nursery rhyme.
5. Discuss the origin of the song and talk about how people paid with products rather than money in historic times.

What's in it for the children?

Not only will the activity teach children about music, rhyme and language, it has a simple storyline that is easy to understand and learn, therefore suitable for young children. By singing and acting out this song children will develop a basic number sense, whilst they can also experience the idea of paying, gifting and sharing.

Midsummer's night

Freeform small worlds

What you need:

- Cotton wool
- Shaving foam
- Fresh and/or dry flowers
- Glitter
- Earth, moss
- Bark pieces
- Small cardboard box
- Fairy and people play figures
- Children's version of *A Midsummer Night's Dream* by William Shakespeare

What's in it for the children?

Children can experience a historic variation of English language when reading Shakespeare. They can study human life and gain experience of how some events in our lives cannot be influenced or controlled.

Taking it forward

- Provide dressing-up clothes related to the original story.
- Create background scenes using only one type of material such as fabric, natural objects, monochrome things like aluminium foil.

Observation questions

- Can the children understand the difference between imagination and reality?
- Do the children have some understanding of languages being different all over the world?

What to do:

1. Tell *A Midsummer Night's Dream* to the children using a children's version of the Shakespeare story. Give them some short extracts from the original text too to get a flavour of the Elizabethan English.
2. Divide the uses area (such as the table) into three different sections to create a fairy home, a theatre and a forest.
3. In the fairy home place cotton wool and shaving foam and cover with glitter and fresh flowers.
4. For the theatre, take the top off a small cardboard box and create a caved stage by standing the box on its side.
5. Arrange the bark pieces, earth and moss to create a forest.
6. Introduce the fairy and people toy figures and encourage the children to act out parts of the story.
7. Practise old English words.

Harvest

Freeform small worlds

What you need:

- A large piece of dark card for background
- Storybook *The Little Red Hen*
- Mouse
- Dog
- Cat
- Wheat stalks
- Barley
- Rice
- Brown playdough
- Wooden dollhouse furniture

What's in it for the children?

Small worlds are open-ended, and there are many ways a child can play with and experience them. This small world scene allows children to change the way they interact with the world as time goes by, based on experiences they need to process their own life events and what they find important in their own lives.

Taking it forward

- Use the same small world set up to create completely new harvest stories.

Observation questions

- Can the children retell and invent stories?
- Do the children reorganise and personalise the scene?

What to do:

1. Set up the base: lay the large piece of card on the table.
2. Take some of the rice and barley mixture and spread it on the surface.
3. Spread some brown playdough into one area of the base, with the wheat stalks 'planted' in the playdough.
4. Now add the doll's house furniture (a couch, a dinner table and chairs, a stove).
5. Finally add the animals, read *The Little Red Hen* then discuss the story.
6. Encourage them to retell the story of *The Little Red Hen*, make up their own version of the story or change parts of it.
7. Plant the wheat.
8. Encourage children to engage with the sensory parts of the world, for example run their fingers through the rice and barley mixture.
9. Use the small world to tell completely new stories.

Bear hunt

Freeform small worlds

What you need:

- A large, dark card for background
- Chalk
- Play people
- Green tissue paper
- A bowl of water
- A bowl of earth
- A bowl of flour
- Sticks
- A shoebox
- Play paper bear
- Storybook *We're Going on a Bear Hunt* by Michael Rosen

What to do:

1. Set up the base: lay the large card and draw a house on the edge of the circle.
2. Place in the toy people.
3. Draw a short arrow from the house to the next station, which will be grass, following the bear hunt story.
4. The next station will be the bowl of water (representing the river), then the earth (representing the mud), then the sticks (representing the forest), followed by the flour (representing the snow), finally, the shoebox, representing the bear cave.
5. Place the toy bear into the shoebox.
6. Read the story *We're Going on a Bear Hunt* to the children and encourage them to act out the events in turn.

What's in it for the children?

With its vivid descriptions and continuous onomatopoeia, this story has the potential to send children off through dense forests and over snowy mountains, swimming through lakes and squelching through mud. Acting out the story offers teaching opportunities in language, rhythm, sensory development, social skills and teamwork.

Taking it forward

- Place bear footstep cut outs around the room and hide the bear for excitement. Rewrite the story, replacing the areas with places from the children's play environment, such as 'Oh-oh, a table and chairs. We can't go over it ...' and so on.

Observation questions

- Can the children sense rhythm in texts/words?
- Do the children engage with the sensory elements of this scene?